Butterfield School
Learning Center
1441 W. Lake Street
Libertyville, IL 60048

DEMCO

THE CIVIL WAR
LEADERS AND GENERALS

BY JIM OLLHOFF

Vᴉsɪᴛ ᴜs ᴀᴛ
www.abdopublishing.com

Published by ABDO Publishing Company, PO Box 398166, Minneapolis, MN 55439.

Printed in the United States of America, North Mankato, Minnesota.
112011
012012

PRINTED ON RECYCLED PAPER

Editor: John Hamilton
Graphic Design: John Hamilton
Cover Design: Neil Klinepier
Cover Photo: Getty Images
Interior Photos and Illustrations: Corbis, p. 20-21, 23, 24, 25; Getty Images, p. 4-5, 8, 11, 12-13, 14, 21, 26, 27, 29; Granger, p. 17, 18, 19, 28; Library of Congress, p. 1, 3, 9, 10, 15, 16, 22; Thinkstock, p. 6-7.

ABDO Booklinks

To learn more about the Civil War, visit ABDO Publishing Company online. Web sites about the Civil War are featured on our Book Links pages. These links are routinely monitored and updated to provide the most current information available. Web site: www.abdopublishing.com

Library of Congress Cataloging-in-Publication Data

Ollhoff, Jim, 1959-
  The Civil War : leaders and generals / Jim Ollhoff.
    p. cm. -- (The Civil War)
  Includes index.
  ISBN 978-1-61783-275-8
  1. United States--History--Civil War, 1861-1865--Biography--Juvenile literature. I. Title. II. Title: Leaders and generals.
  E467.O45 2012
  973.7092--dc23
  [B]
                      2011039980

CONTENTS

Officers from the staff of Union General George McClellan in 1862.

The Civil War

LEADERS AND GENERALS

Like most wars, the American Civil War was filled with colorful, complex personalities. Confederate General Robert E. Lee was a brilliant military planner and a polite gentleman.

President Abraham Lincoln was a remarkable leader with a dry sense of humor, but he often suffered from deep sadness. Union General Ulysses S. Grant was a great military leader, but he once resigned from the army, possibly to keep from being court-martialed for drunkenness.

Union General George McClellan was the best trainer of soldiers, but his ineptness on the battlefield prolonged the war. General Winfield Scott, the commander of the Union army at the start of the Civil War, created the strategy that would ultimately doom the South, but he was too out of shape to even get on a horse. One of the wisest, most intelligent men in the United States may have been Frederick Douglass, a former slave.

Wars have many leaders, but behind the scenes there are ordinary people who often go unnoticed. Wives of soldiers knitted uniforms and took care of the farms while the men were away. African American soldiers fought for the Union army with uncommon bravery, but were paid much less than their white counterparts. Doctors and nurses worked tirelessly under terrible conditions. All of these Americans and many more were heroes in their own way. We can all learn from their leadership.

February 12, 1809—April 15, 1865

ABRAHAM LINCOLN

President Abraham Lincoln is one of the most admired men in American history. He was intelligent and compassionate. He kept a steady hand on the nation through the most difficult years in its history. He motivated people, first to preserve the union of the United States, later to end slavery.

Lincoln was born in Hardin County, Kentucky, in 1809. His family moved to Indiana in 1816.

He served in the military for a few years, and then lost an election for the state legislature in 1832. In 1834, he was elected to the Illinois legislature, where he served for eight years. In 1846, he was elected to the U.S. House of Representatives. He took turns practicing law and being involved in politics. He won election for president in 1860, just as the Southern states were seceding from the Union.

The Lincoln
Memorial, in
Washington, D.C.

Union cavalry troops fight Confederate cavalry with sabers during a reenactment of the Battle of Gettysburg at the Gettysburg National Military Park in Pennsylvania.

Historians rate Abraham Lincoln as one of the best presidents in American history. His steady leadership kept the nation together. That leadership is clear in a speech he gave on November 19, 1863. Today the speech is called the Gettysburg Address. Lincoln was helping dedicate the Soldiers' National Cemetery in Gettysburg, Pennsylvania, almost five months after the Battle of Gettysburg, one of the turning points of the war.

Lincoln's speech at Gettysburg lasted only a few minutes, but it is perhaps the most famous speech in American history:

"Four score and seven years ago our fathers brought forth, upon this continent, a new nation, conceived in liberty, and dedicated to the proposition that "all men are created equal."

"Now we are engaged in a great civil war, testing whether that nation, or any nation so conceived, and so

dedicated, can long endure. We are met on a great battlefield of that war. We have come to dedicate a portion of it, as a final resting place for those who died here, that the nation might live. This we may, in all propriety do.

"But, in a larger sense, we can not dedicate—we can not consecrate—we can not hallow, this ground. The brave men, living and dead, who struggled here, have hallowed it, far above our poor power to add or detract. The world will little note, nor long remember what we say here; while it can never forget what they did here.

"It is rather for us, the living, we here be dedicated to the great task remaining before us—that, from these honored dead we take increased devotion to that cause for which they here, gave the last full measure of devotion—that we here highly resolve these dead shall not have died in vain; that the nation, shall have a new birth of freedom, and that government of the people, by the people, for the people, shall not perish from the Earth."

Lincoln was reelected for a second term as president in 1864. In his speech at his second inauguration on March 4, 1865, he laid out his plans for rebuilding the nation:

"With malice toward none; with charity for all; with firmness in the right, as God gives us to see the right, let us strive on to finish the work we are in; to bind up the nation's wounds..."

Tragically, Lincoln was killed by an assassin's bullet six weeks later, just days after the end of the Civil War. His family tomb is in Springfield, Illinois.

President Abraham Lincoln in 1865.

June 3, 1808—December 6, 1889

JEFFERSON DAVIS

Jefferson Davis was president of the Confederacy during the Civil War. He was born in Kentucky in 1808. He attended the United States Military Academy at West Point, New York, where officers are trained. He fought in the Black Hawk War of 1832 and in the Mexican-American War (1846-1848).

Davis served as the United States Secretary of War under President Franklin Pierce. After Davis was elected to the Senate for the state of Mississippi, he became a fierce defender of the South. He spoke out in favor of slavery, which he called "African servitude." He was narrow-minded and stubborn, and inflexible in his ideas. His staff and cabinet bickered endlessly.

Jefferson Davis accepted the nomination to become the president of the Confederacy on February 18, 1861, but that put him in a difficult position. The Confederacy was built on the idea that the states were independent, and yet he was president of the Confederacy's central government. So, anything he did for the states as a whole, even calling for an army, was viewed with suspicion by the individual states.

*A portrait of
Jefferson Davis
taken in 1865.*

When the South surrendered in
1865, he was captured in Georgia
and thrown in jail—without a
trial—for two years. After he was
released from prison he went to
Canada. He eventually returned and
wrote a history of the Confederate
states. He died in 1889, and is
buried in Richmond, Virginia.

January 19, 1807 – October 12, 1870

GENERAL ROBERT E. LEE

Confederate General Robert E. Lee was born in Westmoreland County, Virginia, into a military family. His father, Henry Lee, was the governor of Virginia and a hero of the Revolutionary War (1775-1783).

Robert E. Lee graduated from the United States Military Academy at West Point, New York, in 1829. He spent many years as a combat engineer, supervising the construction of coastal defenses.

From 1852 to 1855, Lee was the superintendent of West Point. This meant that he was in charge of training and preparing many officers who would later serve under him, and serve against him, during the Civil War.

In 1861, President Abraham Lincoln asked Robert E. Lee to be the commander of the Union army. Although Lee did not agree with slavery or the South's secession, he could not bring himself to fight against his home state of Virginia.

Lee declined the president's offer and resigned his commission in the army. He then became a general in the Confederate army.

A Civil War reenactor playing Robert E. Lee rides a horse during a reenactment of the Battle of Gettysburg in Gettysburg, Pennsylvania.

Lee was the Civil War's best strategist. He was good at reasoning what the opposing generals were going to do, and then designing a way to stop the enemy forces. He made excellent use of reconnaissance information, and knew his generals. Despite being constantly outnumbered, he almost always inflicted huge damage on the enemy. His soldiers loved him and would do almost anything for him. Even after the war, his fame as a brilliant military strategist rose, in the North as well as the South.

In 1864, the Union army had filled their cemeteries and needed a new place to bury their dead. A quartermaster general who hated the Confederates chose the new cemetery: the grounds of Robert E. Lee's house in Arlington County, Virginia. Lee's old homestead became today's Arlington National Cemetery.

After the war, in 1865 Lee became the president of Washington College in Lexington, Virginia. He served there until he

General Robert E. Lee (holding binoculars) leading the Confederate victory at the Battle of Fredericksburg, Virginia, in 1862.

had a stroke in 1870. He died two weeks later, on October 12, 1870. The college then changed its name to Washington and Lee University. Lee is buried beneath the chapel at the university.

Robert E. Lee was a quiet, polite Southern gentleman. After the war, he encouraged the North and South to make amends and live peaceably. He handled his life, both during and after the war, with quiet dignity and honor.

A portrait of Confederate General Robert E. Lee, taken in 1864.

April 27, 1822—July 23, 1885

GENERAL ULYSSES S. GRANT

Union General Ulysses S. Grant was born in Point Pleasant, Ohio, as Hiram Ulysses Grant. When he was accepted to the United States Military Academy at West Point, New York, in 1839, he was mistakenly enrolled as Ulysses S. Grant, a name that he kept. People described him as slouching and slovenly.

He fought in the Mexican-American War (1846–1848), and distinguished himself for bravery. He was transferred to Fort Humboldt in California, far from his family. His despair at missing his family and an unpleasant commanding officer drove him to alcohol. He resigned from the army in 1854.

At the outbreak of the Civil War, Grant began to recruit and train soldiers in Illinois. He was reinstated into the ranks, and was soon promoted to general.

In 1863, Grant led the Union army to a victory at Vicksburg, Mississippi. The battle was one of the turning points of the war. Grant won so many battles that people said the initials "U.S." in his name stood for "Unconditional Surrender."

General Ulysses S.
Grant at his Cold Harbor,
Virginia, headquarters
in 1864.

General Ulysses S. Grant (center, on brown horse with saber) directing a charge at the Battle of Shiloh, Tennessee, in April 1862. The battle was a Union victory, but thousands of soldiers from both sides lost their lives.

Many generals in the Civil War only knew how to charge. But Grant knew when to charge and when to retreat, when to wait and when to march around to the other side of the enemy. He had an uncanny knack for strategy—for knowing what to do to defeat the Confederate forces.

In March 1864, Grant was appointed lieutenant general, which meant he was in charge of all the armies of the Union forces. He knew that the Confederate army was dwindling from lack of food, money, and supplies. Grant's plan was to pound the Confederate forces mercilessly. He cut off Confederate supply lines, stopped or captured reinforcements, and split the enemy forces into isolated pieces.

In April 1865, Confederate General Robert E. Lee surrendered

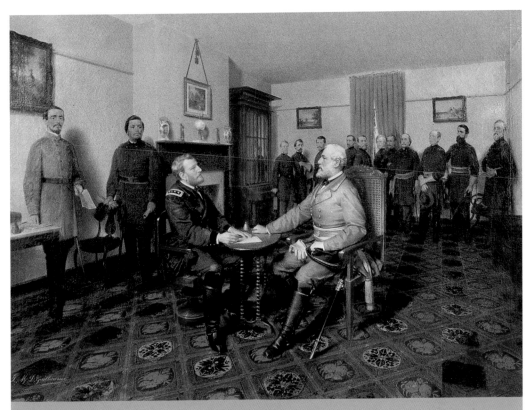

General Grant (seated, at left) accepts the surrender of Confederate General Robert E. Lee at Appomattox Court House, Virginia, on April 9, 1865.

to General Grant at the village of Appomattox Court House, Virginia. Grant was cordial to Lee, and made sure that General Lee's troops were fed and treated properly. Grant wrote later how he was sad for Lee, who believed in his cause and fought so valiantly.

Grant was elected president of the United States, and served from 1869–1877. Most historians agree that he was a better general than a president. His presidency was marked by scandal and infighting, which overshadowed some of his accomplishments in civil rights.

Grant died from throat cancer in 1885. He is buried in a large mausoleum in New York City's Riverside Park. Grant's own words are written on his tombstone, "Let us have peace."

January 21, 1824—May 10, 1863

GENERAL THOMAS "STONEWALL" JACKSON

Confederate General Thomas "Stonewall" Jackson was born in Clarksburg, in what today is West Virginia. In 1842, he entered the United States Military Academy at West Point, New York. He graduated in 1846, and was sent by the army to Mexico to fight in the Mexican-American War (1846–1848). After serving in a variety of places, Jackson eventually retired. But in 1861, he joined the Confederate army.

At the 1861 Battle of Bull Run, the first important battle of the war, General Jackson was responsible for protecting a hill from incoming Union forces. In the chaos of the battle, one of the Confederate generals said that Jackson was standing like a "stone wall" against the Union. That nickname stuck, and he became known as Stonewall Jackson.

On March 2, 1863, Jackson was accidentally shot by his own troops during a battle. He was taken to a place to rest, but his condition worsened, and he finally died on May 10.

General Thomas "Stonewall" Jackson

General Jackson was an excellent military strategist. He and General Robert E. Lee made a great team. They always seemed to be in synch, and seemed to know what the other was thinking. Historians wonder how the Civil War would have been different had General Jackson not been killed.

"The Last Meeting of Lee and Jackson" depicts Stonewall Jackson (left) and Robert E. Lee (right) meeting on the battlefield. The painting was created in 1877 by artist J.G. Fay.

December 3, 1826—October 29, 1885

GENERAL
GEORGE McCLELLAN

Union General George McClellan was born in Pennsylvania in 1826. In 1846, he graduated second in his class from the United States Military Academy at West Point, New York. His first military experience was in the Mexican-American War (1846–1848).

At the start of the Civil War, General McClellan began to organize volunteers. In August 1861, he organized the Army of the Potomac, a huge army fighting mainly in Virginia. He became the commander of the Army of the Potomac. In November 1861, President Lincoln appointed him as the general-in-chief of all the armies of the Union.

McClellan was an expert at organizing and training. He knew how to get soldiers ready for battle. However, as a battlefield commander, he was paralyzed with indecision and fear. He constantly overestimated enemy troop sizes. This led him to sit and wait for reinforcements, instead of taking the initiative. He agonized over

George McClellan

decisions to attack, and often disobeyed Lincoln's orders to attack Confederate positions. When he had a military advantage, McClellan didn't capitalize. In March 1862, President Lincoln removed McClellan from his position as general-in-chief.

In 1864, McClellan ran for president against Abraham Lincoln. McClellan promised voters that he would immediately stop the war and recognize the Confederacy as its own nation. However, Abraham Lincoln was re-elected in a landslide.

In 1878, McClellan became the governor of New Jersey. He wrote several books, including material on the Civil War defending his actions. He died in 1885, and is buried in Trenton, New Jersey.

1820?—March 10, 1913

HARRIET TUBMAN

Harriet Tubman was born a slave in Maryland around 1820. Her given name was Araminta Ross, but she later took her mother's name, Harriet, and her husband's last name, Tubman. In 1849, she heard rumors that she was about to be sold, but she escaped slavery and fled to Philadelphia, Pennsylvania.

The next year, Tubman secretly made her way back to Maryland, and then helped her sister and two children escape slavery. This was the first of many trips she would take to lead more than 300 slaves to freedom. She was a conductor on the Underground Railroad. This "railroad" was not a railroad at all, but a series of secret routes and safe houses where slaves were led to freedom.

During the Civil War, Tubman served as a nurse and a scout for Union forces. She even led a group of Union soldiers into Confederate territory, the Combahee River Raid, to seize supplies and set black slaves free. After the Civil War, she set up homes for elderly and poor African Americans and worked to support the right of women to vote. She died of pneumonia in 1913, and is buried in Auburn, New York.

Harriet Tubman had remarkable courage to make so many trips into slave areas. Many rewards were offered for her capture. But she was creative and persistent, and helped others develop the courage needed to work for justice and freedom. Her life continues to inspire those who fight for equality, justice, and civil rights.

Harriet Tubman (right, in blue dress) escorting escaped slaves to Canada.

25

FREDERICK DOUGLASS

Frederick Douglass was born a slave on a Maryland plantation, probably sometime in 1817 or 1818. He didn't know his exact birthday, but chose to celebrate it as February 14. He never knew his white father, and he was separated from his mother when he was an infant. His grandmother raised him. He learned to read, and escaped slavery in 1838. He fled to New York City, and later to Massachusetts.

In 1841, there was an anti-slavery convention in Nantucket, Massachusetts. Douglass was asked to speak about slavery and his experience. He spoke so powerfully about the horrors of slavery that he was instantly in demand as a speaker.

Some people at that time believed the racist idea that Africans were not as intelligent as whites. They said Fredrick Douglass could not possibly have been a slave, because he was too smart.

In response to this criticism, Douglass wrote an autobiography, *Narrative of the Life of Frederick Douglass, An American Slave,* detailing his experiences as a slave. Published in 1845, it became a classic of American literature.

Frederick Douglass

A mob and police break up an abolitionist meeting in Boston, Massachusetts, December 3, 1860, as Frederick Douglass (center) tries to speak.

Douglass began to work with the popular abolitionist William Lloyd Garrison, but they later disagreed on the best tactics to end slavery. Douglass went on a speaking tour in England, Scotland, and Ireland. When he came back to the United States, he started an anti-slavery newspaper called *The North Star*. Later, it became known as *Frederick Douglass' Paper*.

During the Civil War, President Abraham Lincoln often requested Douglass's wisdom and used him as a consultant and advisor. Douglass pushed for the Union to use black soldiers in the war.

After the Civil War, he supported women's rights, and pushed for their right to vote. He held several positions in the government, including minister and consul general to Haiti in 1889–1891. He was the first African American to hold a high position in the United States government.

Frederick Douglass believed in the equality of all people, and

Frederick Douglass (right) urges President Abraham Lincoln (seated left) to allow African Americans to fight in the Union army during the Civil War.

believed that everyone should be treated with dignity and honor. He continued to educate himself all of his life.

Douglass lived during a troubled time, when voices were needed to right wrongs and correct injustices.

Through his writing, speaking, and wisdom, he was a powerful influence for good.

Frederick Douglass died on February 20, 1895, probably of a heart attack. He is buried in Rochester, New York.

GLOSSARY

ABOLITIONISTS

A person who opposed slavery.

CIVIL WAR

A war where two parts of the same nation fight against each other. The American Civil War was fought between Northern and Southern states from 1861–1865. The Southern states were for slavery. They wanted to start their own country. Northern states fought against slavery and a division of the country.

CONFEDERACY

The Southern states of Alabama, Arkansas, Florida, Georgia, Louisiana, Mississippi, North Carolina, South Carolina, Tennessee, Texas, and Virginia. These states wanted to keep slavery legal. They broke away from the United States during the Civil War and formed their own country known as the Confederate States of America, or the Confederacy. The Confederacy ended in 1865 when the war ended and the 11 Confederate states rejoined the United States.

EMANCIPATION PROCLAMATION

President Lincoln's declaration issued on January 1, 1863, that freed the slaves. The word emancipation means to be set free. For many African Americans, emancipation after the Civil War meant freedom from slavery.

PLANTATION

A large farm where crops such as tobacco, sugar cane, and cotton are grown. Workers usually live right on the property. Early plantation owners in North America used cheap slave labor to make their operations more profitable.

RACISM

The belief that people of one skin color are better than a people of another skin color, or that individuals of a certain skin color have certain characteristics *because* of their skin color.

RECONNAISSANCE

A military observation of an area in order to locate the enemy or determine a potential battlefield's strengths and weaknesses.

SECEDE

To withdraw membership in a union or alliance.

UNCONDITIONAL SURRENDER

A surrender with no conditions or terms, in which the losing side must give up fighting immediately and be at the total mercy of the winning side.

UNDERGROUND RAILROAD

A large network of secret routes and safe houses that worked to transport runaway slaves to freedom in the Northern states or Canada.

UNION

The Northern states, who were united against the Confederacy. "Union" also refers to all of the states of the United States. President Lincoln wanted to preserve the Union, keeping the Northern and Southern states together.

INDEX